D1450316

THE BROKEN CURSE

THE BROKEN CURSE

Gaining Freedom from Hurtful Words

Tom Elliff

PUBLICATIONS

Fort Washington, PA 19034

The Broken Curse
Published by CLC Publications

U.S.A.
P.O. Box 1449, Fort Washington, PA 19034

UNITED KINGDOM
CLC International (UK)
Unit 5, Glendale Avenue, Sandycroft, Flintshire, CH5 2QP

Printed in the United States of America

ISBN (paperback): 978-1-61958-241-5
ISBN (e-book): 978-1-61958-242-2

Contents

Prologue 7

1　The Curse 9

2　"I've Got One!" 17

3　Believe in the Awesome Power
　　of the Spoken Word. 25

4　Beware of the Awful Problem
　　with the Spoken Word 35

5　The Curse That Is Already Broken 45

6　His Word. 51

7　His Name 57

8　His Blood. 63

9　Breaking the Curse of Words 69

10　My Appeal. 79

　　Epilogue. 85

Prologue

THE ROOM WHERE I USUALLY WRITE has an expansive view across a lightly forested area that hosts the confluence of two creeks. All kinds of wildlife abound in that area, some feathered, some furry, and some with human skin. The local children, including my own grandchildren, love to play down by the water beneath the trees. Because of this, Jeannie and I have an assortment of shoes at our back entry, none of which fit us, but most of which are covered with mud that will have to be removed before they can be worn again.

It's difficult to walk in muddy shoes. I know from experience that it can be tiring, down right aggravating, in fact. Muddy shoes weigh you down and make progress slow and cumbersome.

Perhaps your life has become just as difficult. You are weighed down with the accumulated disappointments, failures and verbal clods of the past. Rather than your life being a heady adventure, you are just slogging it out. Isn't it time you removed the verbal debris that has accumulated on your soul?

Isn't it time you experienced what it means to run again, unhindered? I want to invite you on a personal journey into a life set free from the curse of hurtful, painful and destructive words. To be quite honest, I do not *think* the liberating truth in this small book will work for you. I *know* it will! I know this truth will set you free because God's Word assures us that it will. But I also know about this freedom through personal experience. You see, this book is the story of my personal deliverance.

1

The Curse

"Face it," he snorted. The worn swivel chair behind his desk seemed to creak in affirmation as my friend leaned backwards toward a cluttered credenza. A smile traced across the older man's wizened face as he nodded his head with an air of knowing confidence. "You're just like me and everyone else I know. That's why I can say with certainty that you will never succeed. I haven't mastered that spiritual discipline and neither will you, so just get used to it."

With a dismissive wave of his hand he turned his attention back to some papers on his desk, indicating that our discussion was over. Because I held this man in high esteem, I left his office with the assumption that his judgment of my spiritual passion must be correct. Worse yet, I walked away that day quietly resigned to a lifetime of frustration in an important area of my spiritual life. After all, as he had said, I was "just like him."

THE SEAMS IN THE CONCRETE HIGHWAY beat a steady rhythm beneath the wheels of the small blue sedan as I drove eastward across Oklahoma toward the Arkansas state line. Behind me the setting sun was accompanying the highway's beat with an ever-changing kaleidoscope of color, viewed only in part by an occasional glance at the rearview mirror. The repetitive sound of the wheels on the highway was almost hypnotic, serving only to punctuate five phrases I sought to dismiss from my mind.

"You're just like me!"

"You will never . . . "

"If God ever takes His hand off a man, He never . . . !"

"What do you think you're doing?"

"It's too late for you!"

Somehow, the vibrations of the highway seemed to be jarring those long-forgotten statements loose from their hiding places, each one accompanied with its painful recollection of repeated failure.

I was perplexed. Why was it that, in spite of all the positive and encouraging statements I'd heard over the years, those five negative statements were so deeply and indelibly etched in my spirit? Though spoken years and miles away, they were as fresh in my mind as if uttered only minutes earlier. Was it because of my love and respect for those who'd spoken those words to me? Was it the place, or time, when they were spoken? The look in the person's eyes? The tone of voice? The shock I'd felt when hearing them, almost as if I'd been hit with a physical blow? Was it because those statements were made at a moment when I was particularly vulnerable? Perhaps that had been the cause for the enduring impact of those words.

But then I recalled that, on at least one occasion, I was simply listening in on a conversation among three men for whom I had great admiration. One of the men made a statement that I had subsequently drawn into my heart much the same as an unwitting victim inhales passive smoke. Now those words continued to silently infect my spirit with a deadly malignancy.

Here was the irony: I actually despised all five of those statements, or at least the picture of defeat and failure they painted on the walls of my heart. Yet, in spite of all my best efforts, they had become self-fulfilling prophecies. Those words were like a curse to me. It seemed the harder I tried *not* to fulfill them, the more they were becoming like an autopilot, subconsciously guiding my behavior unless I deliberately took control over them.

Reflecting back, I recalled that I was not alone in dealing with the pain and defeat brought on by the curse of words. I remembered the distressed wife who asked how she should encourage her husband to experience the thrill of singing in worship. While still in elementary school, his teacher had asked him to refrain from singing with the choir at a rehearsal for the class's Christmas presentation. "I think you're singing off-key," the teacher had said, almost as an aside. "He clammed up," his wife now lamented, "and he inwardly resolved never to sing again." Now that man was fifty-five years of age and a successful businessman, but the memory of his teacher's words was robbing him of the joy of song.

And there was the seminary student who once confessed that, though he loved every aspect of ministry, he knew he would never be a successful pastor. "You're nothing but a big old dumb 'galoot,'" his father had repeatedly hissed in anger and disdain as he looked with disgust on his growing son's lanky frame. "And I've just always assumed he was right," the student had said to me with an air of resignation.

With sadness I recalled how, on more than one occasion, some bright, normally energetic, and relatively young mother would inform me that her husband and the father of her children was dissatisfied with their marriage. "I think he's infatuated with someone at the office, or down at the gym where he works out," she would say, shoulders sagging with grief and resignation. Then she would tell how her husband would repeatedly mock her for the sags and stretch marks that always seemed to reappear with renewed vengeance with the arrival of each successive child.

"He tells me that I've just let myself go, and I guess he's right. Anyway, pastor," she would sigh, "I've got to go pick up the kids at school, get them to their lessons, prepare dinner, get the house straightened up and the kids to bed before he gets home from the gym. He likes things to be quiet when he comes home from a hard day at work."

I could only imagine what verbal compass was now guiding that weary wife's behavior. What picture of their future married life had been painted on the walls of her heart by the tongue of her spiritually immature and disgruntled husband?

With my destination only a few miles ahead, I wondered if there was any way for me to break free from what I later began to call the curse of words. James spoke of the reality of such a curse when writing about the importance of using our tongue properly. Pointing to the evil inconsistency inherent in our speech, he notes that with our tongue "we bless our Lord and Father, and with it we *curse* men, who have been made in the likeness of God" (James 3:9). The wheels of my car crunched over the gravel-covered parking lot adjacent to the small church where I was to speak that evening. I was relieved to see people still walking from their vehicles toward the building that was now bathed in the yellow glow of a single large bulb positioned directly over the double-doored entrance. From the looks of the vehicles in the parking lot—mostly trucks—it appeared we'd have a great crowd.

Before opening my car door, I placed both hands on the steering wheel, took a deep breath and made a solemn resolution. Once my assignment was over and I was making the return trip home, I was going to prayerfully and fervently seek God's answer for my dilemma. It was time for me to break the curse of those words that were so negatively impacting my life. By God's grace, I was going to wrestle this problem to the ground.

A screeching symphony of cicadas greeted me as I opened the door of the car. Only recently set free from their interminable earthly imprisonment, they were now enjoying a noisy and unembarrassed courtship. Planting both feet on the ground, I filled my lungs with the hot, dry summer air. It was now time to turn my attention to the purpose for my visit. As we say in Oklahoma, this was "meetin' time."

Though I remember little of the meeting, I do recall the eagerness with which I anticipated the drive back home that evening. As soon as proper decorum permitted, I said my goodbyes to the friendly crowd and the local pastors, walked to my car, and drove off toward home.

"Father," I prayed, "the desire of my heart is to gain victory over the curse of those words spoken years ago and miles away. Will You teach me tonight? Will You show me how to break free? Will You show me how to use the weapons of warfare that are not carnal but spiritual?" Those were the words on my lips as I eased my car out of the parking lot, drove through the small town, steered up an entry ramp and onto the interstate. For the next three hours, God had a captive audience.

That summer night, I discovered the secret that sets us free from what I have come to call the "curse of words"—the lingering, hurtful consequences of statements that, even now, continue to negatively impact our lives. With God's answer, and the freedom I now enjoy, there has come the requirement that I share this secret with you. Good stewardship of the truth demands it!

On the following pages you will read about God's secret for breaking the curse of words. My use of the word secret is not a reference to something heretofore restricted from view and only now revealed. Generally speaking, what's true is not new. Instead, I am using the term secret to speak of God's clearly defined answer, His key that opens the door and sets you free from the curse of words. What you will discover in these pages is that God has a strategy for successfully confronting the effect of any words that are shaping your life in a manner contrary to His wonderful plan.

For some who read this, it will come as a welcome surprise to discover that the curse has already been broken, and all that remains is for you to employ the simple strategy and powerful tools that have been placed at your disposal. That was true in my case and may be true in yours as well.

But first, you are invited to our home on the night following my remarkable discovery. Come sit with me at our dinner table and listen to a sobering conversation.

2

"I've Got One!"

"It happened when we were living in Africa," my youngest daughter explained. "You had spent the better part of the day attempting to connect by phone with someone in the States. Coming home from school on my bicycle, I rolled over a cobra snake in our driveway and rushed in to tell you about it. You kept placing your finger over your mouth, attempting to hear the person on the phone. But the more you tried to shush me and calm me down, the more animated I became. When your conversation was ended, you hung up the phone in disgust, turned toward me, blurted out my name and said, "I could just shoot you!"

MUCH SOONER THAN EXPECTED, I was easing the car up our driveway and into the dimly lit garage. I was eager to share with my wife, Jeannie, the details of what was, quite plainly, a meeting with God. Out on the highway, the Lord had unfolded to me His strategy for breaking the curse of words. I had called to mind passages of Scripture that I had frequently studied over the years, passages that had become like old friends to me. God began speaking to me by His Spirit and through His Word, the Bible. He revealed His plan, step by step, until it was clear what I must do. But after every piece of the plan had finally fallen in place, it seemed that God had grown silent.

A friend of mine was accustomed to saying, "When God is silent, that means it's your move!" I knew God was waiting for me to apply this newly discovered strategy to the five statements that had become like a curse to me. With a trembling heart and voice, I began. Carefully following the plan God had so clearly shown me in His Word, I brought each statement before the Lord.

It would be difficult for me to describe the personal sense of revival, freedom and joy in the Lord that I experienced that evening as the car, seemingly self-guided, rolled through the night toward home. At first I began worshiping the Lord, virtually shouting His praises as the tears rolled down my cheeks. Then I began to sing—first some songs I remembered, and then some new songs from remembered verses of Scripture that seemed to flow up from deep within my heart, spilling over with joy and laughter. God had indeed broken the curse of those words in my life, and by the time I arrived home my voice was literally hoarse from shouting and singing praises to the Lord.

"You will never believe what God has shown me," I said to Jeannie while settling into bed beside her. Though it was well past midnight, I was energized by my newly discovered truth and wanted to talk.

Looking back, I suppose that I fully expected Jeannie to sit straight up in bed, eyes wide open with excitement, take pen and notebook in hand and begin recording my insights.

That's not the way it happened! Weary from the previous day's activities, and having been now awakened from a deep sleep, Jeannie turned toward me with half-closed eyes and mumbled, "I'm not sure I can concentrate, so do you think it can wait until breakfast?"

"I guess it'll have to," I replied, putting my hands behind my head and gazing up at the ceiling with a smile. "Boy!" I thought to myself, "Will that ever be an interesting discussion!"

The short night, coupled with the need to get the younger children to school on time, didn't provide the kind of setting I wanted in order to share my thoughts. So I quickly came up with an alternate plan that, in the end, proved to be even better than imagined.

"Tonight," I said to the family, now seated at the breakfast table, "I will have some very important news to share at dinner. Everybody needs to be at the table on time. No exceptions!"

I refused to cave in to the pleas of either my wife or children to at least give them some hint regarding the secret, so by dinner everyone was eager to hear the news. Our eldest daughter, only recently engaged, had encouraged her fiancé to join us for the meal. (Actually, I was beginning to realize that, when it came to excuses for the two of them to be together, he didn't need much encouragement at all!) I let the suspense continue to build through the mealtime. Finally, when dinner was over, I said, "I want to tell you a story."

Slowly, but with obvious excitement, I shared with my family the events of the previous evening. The most difficult part of the story was my confession regarding the negative impact of those five statements on my life. I wasn't certain that anyone would understand or identify with the impact of those statements, especially our children, three of whom were still in their teens.

My fears were confirmed when I finished my story. Each member of my family seemed deep in thought, looking first at me and then down at the table in what I interpreted as embarrassed silence. "They don't get it," I thought to myself. "Maybe this is just one of those truths God wants me to hide in my heart."

"I've got one." The silence was broken by one of my daughters. All eyes turned her way. "Do you remember our family reunion a couple of years ago, and when I accidentally kicked the coffee table, causing a porcelain figurine to fall and shatter? Well, someone, I really don't recall who, blurted out that I was 'the clumsiest person in the world.' Those words really hurt my feelings at the moment. I was so embarrassed. And then those words just seemed to stick in my mind. Now, when I'm around other people I just constantly worry that I'll do something clumsy."

I was astounded at my daughter's admission, especially since that very year she had been elected as homecoming queen in high school! But my daughter's openness prompted the others around the table, including my future son-in-law, to do the same. Negative and hurtful statements that for some reason had found a permanent home in their hearts came tumbling out in an unexpected manner.

"You only have friends because you're the pastor's daughter." My eldest daughter spoke up, identifying a statement made by a grade school friend. She explained how from that point onward, she had tried hard to make certain that her friends were not just "church friends," sometimes with really hurtful consequences.

"'You will never amount to anything.' My father would often repeat those words to me when he was angry and frustrated over something I had done, or done poorly," said my wife tearfully. "For a while I just tried to ignore those words and forgive my daddy, but over time I developed a very poor and unhealthy self-image."

"The good times start when you show up." My son shared how these words, often repeated by his friends, had actually put an unbearable burden on his shoulders. "I know that, in order to live up to those words, I have done some things that would not meet your approval—or God's."

Every person around the table opened up their hearts that evening, sharing statements that had also become like a curse to them. My daughter's fiancé even told of some words that had left him feeling inferior among his peers. The atmosphere was relaxed enough that we actually teased each other a bit, knowing all the while that, underneath everything, we were still dealing with a life-changing issue.

But it was my youngest daughter's openness about that day in Africa that caught me by surprise and provided a living illustration of the negative manner in which we often use our tongue. I will never forget what my daughter said because, in this instance, I was unquestionably the offending party. My irritation over her insistent behavior, coupled with the words, "I could just shoot you," had left an indelible picture in her heart. I could only hang my head in shocked embarrassment at the memory of that moment.

"Daddy," my daughter said, seeing I was on the verge of tears, "I know that's just something people say and that you really didn't mean it. And I've tried to erase that moment from my mind. But I have thought of it so often, and at the strangest times."

By now I was in obvious grief over my callous statement and urged my daughter to forgive me. Sensing the impact her admission had on me, my daughter lovingly assured me that she had "dealt" with the issue, though admittedly she often wondered why it was that she could still so clearly recall those hurtful words.

If you had been physically present around our family's dinner table that evening, you would have heard me carefully explain to my family what God was teaching me about the "curse of words." We would have gladly included you in our circle of prayer as we joined hands and employed the strategy God had shown me the night before. You would have sensed, without question, the air of victory and celebration that followed our time of prayer. And, like the members of my family, you could look back on that moment as the time when God set you free from the curse of words.

But you weren't there. And that's why, in the following pages, I'm inviting you to explore God's secret for breaking the curse of words. You can be set free!

On the next few pages, I'm going to ask you to believe in something, to beware of something, and finally, to break something.

3

Believe in the Awesome Power of the Spoken Word

In "The Whisper Test," Mary Ann Bird tells how she was born with multiple birth defects: deaf in one ear, a cleft palate, a disfigured face, a crooked nose and lopsided feet. As a child, Mary Ann suffered not only these physical impairments but also the emotional damage inflicted by other children. "Oh, Mary Ann," her classmates would say, "what happened to your lip?" "I cut it on a piece of glass," she would lie.

One of her worst experiences at school, she reported, was the day of the annual hearing test. The teacher would call each child to her desk, and the child would cover first one ear and then the other. The teacher would whisper something to the child like "The sky is blue" or "You have new shoes." This was "the whisper test"; if the teacher's phrase was heard and re-peated, the child passed the test. To avoid the humiliation of failure, Mary Ann would always cheat on the test, secretly cupping her hand over her one good ear so that she could still hear what the teacher said.

One year Mary Ann was in the class of Miss Leonard, one of the most beloved and popular teachers in the school. Every student, including Mary Ann, wanted to be noticed by her, wanted to be her pet. Then came the day of the dreaded hearing test. When her turn came, Mary Ann was called to the teacher's desk. As Mary Ann cupped her hand over her good ear, Miss Leonard leaned forward to whisper.

"I waited for those words," Mary Ann wrote, "that God must have put into her mouth, those seven words that changed my life."

Miss Leonard did not say to Mary Ann, "The sky is blue" or "You have new shoes." What she whispered was, "I wish you were my little girl."

TUCKED AWAY IN THE SCRIPT of a nineteenth-century play by Edward Bulwer-Lytton is the statement that "the pen is mightier than the sword." With those words, now so often quoted, the author impressed upon his audience the simple fact that words have awesome power. Words, more than anything else, have the incredible ability to shape both nations and lives. It is not merely the written word that contains such awesome power, but the spoken word as well. Think about it! In the first chapter of Genesis, we discover that our universe, including this world and everything in it, was literally spoken into existence by God. And in the fourth Gospel, when seeking the best means of describing the Creator Himself, the Holy Spirit inspired John to write of Jesus as the "Word," or the sublime physical expression of God who became flesh that He might dwell with us.

Words have power! In recognition of this often-ignored reality, the *Reader's Digest* has for many years used a simple game in its feature "It Pays to Increase Your Word Power" to emphasize to its subscribers that word choice is important. Political pollster, Frank Luntz, takes the thought a step further in his book *Words That Work*, reminding readers that it's not simply what we say that counts, it all boils down to what people hear and understand us to say.

There can be little question that words, written or spoken, have amazing power. The often-quoted saw, "Sticks and stones may break my bones, but words can never hurt me," is, in reality, far from the truth. Words can bless, but they can also do powerful harm. In the New Testament book of James, we are given two pictures that vividly illustrate how the spoken word can affect our lives: a bit placed in the mouth of a horse and the rudder of a great ship.

"Now if we put the bits into the horses' mouths so that they will obey us," writes James, "we direct their entire body as well" (3:3). This picture graphically portrays the manner in which words, like the small appliance placed in the mouth of a large horse, can be used to exert control over others.

Early on, parents learn how to exert control over a child's behavior by the use of certain words. I've sometimes wondered, for instance, how many people, now struggling with obesity, were first led to eat absolutely everything before them with the words "After all, think of all the starving people in . . . " Or there is that commonly used and subtle appeal to a rebellious nature in order to get a kiss from a reluctant child: "Don't you dare kiss me!" And many children have been given the indication that parental respect is simply a matter of geography with the words, "As long as you put your feet under my table, you'll obey me!"

On many occasions, as I am sharing in a group setting about breaking the curse of words, someone will relate how their response to words spoken earlier in life has had a negative impact on their enjoyment of musical expression. You've already read of one lady's grief over her husband's refusal to sing. Now read another account that will encourage you with its positive response to the broken curse of words.

"Did you see where I was sitting tonight?" I was surprised by the lady's question and the animated way in which she was asking it. Frankly, I had no idea where she'd been sitting, but, fortunately, she didn't allow me time to respond.

"I was in the choir. Can you believe it?" she continued excitedly. Then she told me that, after hearing me speak the previous evening on "How to Break the Curse of Words," she had dealt with words spoken to her years earlier while in high school by none other than her mother. Passing the room where her daughter was singing along with a popular radio tune, her mother had said, "I hope nobody ever hears you singing like that!" Now, for the first time in many years, this lady had fulfilled her heart's desire to sing in the choir. She had thoroughly enjoyed the experience and even blushed with enthusiasm when telling me that she was now a full-fledged member of the choir.

Of course, words can and should be used to exert a healthy influence over others, leading them to make decisions that impact their lives in a positive fashion. I clearly remember the words of my grandfather, a preacher and expert woodcraftsman, who asked me to hand him a specific tool hanging on the wall of his woodshop. When I reached for the wrong tool, he carefully pointed out the correct one. When I fumbled a bit, seeking the right tool, my grandfather finally noted that I didn't need to worry. "I've already done what was needed with this old screwdriver I'm holding in my hand."

"Tommy," he said, "I didn't use this screwdriver because it was the best tool for the job, but because it was close at hand." Setting the screwdriver aside, he continued. "There are a lot of men out there who are perfectly equipped to perform the mighty works of God. But God will never use them because they won't stay close to His hand. It's the handy tool that God uses."

With those few words, placed gently in my spirit like a bit in the mouth of a horse, my grandfather led me to see the importance of what has now become the lifelong practice of a daily quiet time with God, staying "handy" to Him through prayer and the study of His Word. James' analogy, comparing words to the bit in a horse's mouth, could scarcely be clearer.

James also reminds us that words can be used to establish the course of a person's life in the same way a rudder is used to set the course of a great ship. "Look at the ships also," he writes, "though they are so great and are driven by strong winds, [they] are still directed by a very small rudder wherever the inclination of the pilot desires" (James 3:4).

Dwight L. Moody's name is synonymous with effective preaching, Christian education and missions. Some maintain that Moody is the greatest evangelist of any era in Christian history. Though over one hundred years have passed since his death in 1899, the impact of this one man's life continues today through ministries around the world. When asked about those events that shaped his life, Moody would often recount the power of one sentence, spoken by his friend Henry Varley, a British lay evangelist, in the early years of Moody's ministry: "It remains to be seen what God will do with a man who gives himself up wholly to Him." Moody determined to be just that man! Most likely, Varley little imagined the power of those words when he first spoke them, yet they were used to establish the course of Moody's life.

Too often, however, words can set the course of a person's life in a direction contrary to the will of God. Sitting in a prison compound, I once visited with the youngest inmate of a federal penitentiary I have ever met. Still in his teens, he spoke bluntly about his experience, saying at one point, "It was meant for me to be here." When I asked him to explain that statement, he related how just a few years earlier his mother had brought him to visit his father who was at that time incarcerated in the very same penitentiary. Looking pensively across the prison yard, the young man said, "My father used to say that I was just like him and that I'd end up here myself one day. And my dad was right!" His father's few thoughtless words had become like the rudder of a great ship, powerfully establishing the course of his son's life.

Words have awesome power: the power to exert control over people, and the power to permanently establish the course of their lives as well. That is why we must use our tongue with such caution. I have often said that the tongue is like a brush, dipped in the palette of the heart and then used to paint a picture on the walls of people's minds. Those pictures can be of grand and godly possibilities, tinted with hues of noble character—pictures of great exploits only achievable by the grace of God. Or they can leave on the walls of people's hearts what amounts to little more than mindless, godless, demeaning graffiti—profane smudges that become constant reminders of defeat and hopelessness.

What pictures have been painted on the walls of your heart? What pictures are you painting on the hearts of others? And if the tongue can be used to bless others so profoundly, why is it that so many of us carry in our heart the curse of words? This question brings us to another issue that demands our constant attention.

4

Beware of the Awful Problem with the Spoken Word

An old fable tells of a court servant who was ordered by his king to search the world over and bring back the best thing he could find. Upon his return, the servant unwrapped a small package before the quizzical king. In it was a tongue. After serious thought, the king commended his servant, saying, "Certainly the tongue has the most wonderful and encouraging power in the world." Then the king ordered his servant to search over the world for the very worst thing he could find and bring it back to him. Soon the servant was back in the courtroom with another small package in which was enclosed—a tongue. "You have done well," said the king, "for the tongue can be as bad as it is good." And this is the picture James paints for us.

"For every species of beasts and birds, of reptiles and creatures of the sea, is tamed and has been tamed by the human race. But no one can tame the tongue; it is a restless evil" (3:7–8).

THAT EVENING AROUND THE DINNER TABLE,
I felt it was important for me to share with my family
each of the five statements that had generated such
long-term and harmful responses on my part. Interest-
ingly, those were certainly not the only negative things
ever said to me or about me—nor even the worst. So
why did those particular words affect me as they did?

I was blessed to be reared in an environment that
was overwhelmingly positive and healthy. If I had a self-
image problem it was probably a matter of overcon-
fidence, and certainly not fear. But each of those five
statements had come to me at a moment of particular vulnerability. They had obviously been spoken at a
time when my normally positive self-image was, for one
reason or another, in question. The "immune system"
of my usually optimistic spirit was obviously in a weak-
ened state and those viral words had just permanently
infected me, periodically surfacing in my memory and
bringing defeat.

I have often wondered about the damage done to
those who live or work in an environment that is almost
never positive. A Christian counselor once told me
that some children actually misbehave in order to get
their parent's attention. "Children thrive on attention,"
he lamented, " and negative attention is better than no

attention at all." But what about the damage done to a child or spouse who receives no attention at all from the most important people in his or her life, unless it is criticism? And how greatly is that damage compounded if the negative atmosphere at home is merely echoed by a similar atmosphere at work or at school? Sadly, many of you who are reading this small book can testify to the emotional and spiritual harm generated in such environments.

It is my experience that words can infect even the most healthy and positive people and become a curse to them. That is because there is a problem—an awful problem—with the tongue. James, the brother of Jesus, sounds like the Lord Himself when he writes about the awful problem with our spoken words. It is a problem we all share. James exclaims, "If anyone does not stumble in what he says, he is a perfect man, able to bridle the whole body as well" (3:2). Then James further describes the problems we have with the spoken word.

There is *iniquity* in the tongue.

"The tongue is a small part of the body," writes James, "and *yet* it boasts of great things. See how great a forest is set aflame by such a small fire! And the tongue is a fire, the *very* world of iniquity" (3:5–6).

Why is there such iniquity—or sin—in our tongue? Because it is tied to our heart! That is why the writer of Proverbs reminds us that the longer we talk, the more likely it is that we will sin in what we say (see 10:19).

Picture your tongue as being something like the mechanical backhoe used on a construction site. Probing from one side to the other, it digs deeper and deeper, turning up what has been long hidden in out-of-sight corners and crevices. Have you ever been on a long bus trip with a group of friends and marveled at the manner in which the conversation began to slide downward until ultimately people were speaking carelessly on the most unseemly topics. That's an illustration of the iniquity that can be hidden in the tongue.

Jesus said that it is out of the abundance of a man's heart that he speaks (see Luke 6:45). If our heart is filled with iniquity—unkind and irreverent thoughts—it will ultimately surface in our speech. My mother was fond of saying that what a man jokes about a little, he thinks about a lot. Or to use a concept popularized in this age of computer science, GIGO—garbage in equals garbage out.

We should fill our minds with the Word of God. Jesus, in fact, reminded us that we are cleansed (trimmed or pruned) by the words He speaks to us (see John 15:3).

Still, in spite of our best efforts, the backhoe of the tongue can dredge up iniquity at the most inopportune moments.

There is *insubordination* in the tongue.

When our family was living in the East African nation of Zimbabwe, big game hunters were fond of saying that no one could tame a Cape buffalo. The Cape buffalo is one of the five most feared animals in Africa. It is large, easily provoked, and when wounded, possesses the ability to escape into the bush and ultimately to begin hunting the hunter. Stories of the fearsome powers of the Cape buffalo abound among longtime safari hunters.

One afternoon, following a particularly successful hunt, some friends and I offered a reward to the man who would capture a Cape buffalo calf. Our intention was to prove that any animal could be tamed, including a Cape buffalo. After the calf was successfully subdued, we placed it in a corral owned by a farmer friend of mine who attempted to tame the small animal by every means possible. He offered the calf sugared water, straw and feed, all to no avail. Ultimately, my exasperated friend reluctantly conceded that every effort to tame the calf only made it more angry and incorrigible. He was finally forced to release the calf into the bush. We concluded that no one could tame a Cape buffalo! Neither can you tame your tongue!

There is never a moment when your tongue has become so domesticated, so trusted, that you can just turn it loose to say whatever you will about others.

There is *infection* in the tongue.

Imagine for a moment that I am holding a large hypodermic syringe just a few feet away from your face. As I push the plunger slightly, a fluid begins oozing out of the needle. I explain to you that the syringe is filled with a deadly, swift-acting virus for which there is no known cure. Moving close to your side, I then ask you to roll up your sleeve so that I might deposit the virus into your arm and beneath your skin. Needless to say, you would violently resist my effort to infect you with the deadly dose contained in the syringe.

But notice that James tells us the tongue is " full of deadly poison" (3:8). This means that you can infect someone with the deadly poisonous venom of your tongue from a great distance. You do not have to touch the body in order to touch a person's heart. Nor does a person have to touch you physically in order to permanently slip deadly and malignant venom into your spirit. It can be done by mere words!

One of the statements that had a negative impact on my life was not actually spoken *to* me, or *about* me, but simply within my hearing. Three men whom I greatly admired were standing by a conveyor belt at an airport, awaiting their luggage. As they stood there, one of the men brought up the name of another who, in spite of great ability, had recently fallen off the radar screen of effectiveness and popularity.

"Well," mused one of my heroes, "it has been my experience that if a man is blessed of God, then loses that blessing, he never receives it again."

I simply sucked that statement into my spiritual lungs where, like a malignant cloud, it began robbing me of spiritual confidence and vitality. It never occurred to me to check that thought out with God through a thorough study of Scripture. After all, this man was a spiritual giant. How could he be wrong?

Later, during a moment of transition in my own ministry from the mission field back to the pastorate, I began seeking the renewed power of God through personal revival.

But that man's statement began echoing in the chambers of my heart. I actually began wondering if my best days of fellowship with God and effectiveness in ministry were all in the past. His statement had become a curse to me. Those words, innocuous as they might have sounded, were filled with deadly poison.

There is *inconsistency* in the tongue.

During my seminary days, a friend and I met at a local course one Friday afternoon for a round of golf. I was eager to visit with my friend who had only recently come to Christ out of a troubled past. One of the great obstacles to his growth in Christ had been the hypocritical attitude expressed by professing Christians. I wanted to show him that, despite the presence of hypocrites in the church, true believers were the "real deal."

As we stood on the tee box, waiting for the foursome in front of us to clear the green, another twosome walked up and asked if they could join us. We thought there would be no problem in letting them do so. After all, the two elderly gentlemen seemed likable enough.

But from his very first shot off the tee, one of the men proved that he possessed a vocabulary that would make a sailor blush. He could not complete a sentence without cursing, and this was only exacerbated by his sorry gamesmanship. His game was so terrible that I even told my partner I was thinking of taking up cursing myself! In addition to his foul language, the man thought he was a comedian, sharing one filthy story after another.

After enduring several minutes of the man's filthy language and crude jokes, I decided to call his hand by asking him what the profession he was in, and then telling him I was a pastor and seminary student.

"Well, I'll be," said the red-faced duffer, "I'm a Christian too!" He then told me of the prestigious church in our community where he served as a deacon alongside a pastor of great repute with whom I was personally acquainted. Dropping his foul language and filthy stories, the man approached every tee with some new example of the manner in which he supported his church and pastor.

"There's a lesson here somewhere, " grinned my friend, "and I don't know whether it's a lesson for me— or for you!

We shouldn't be surprised at the inconsistent use of our tongue. James reminds us that "with it we bless *our* Lord and Father, and with it we curse men, who have been made in the likeness of God; from the same mouth come *both* blessing and cursing" (3:9–10).

"Not even nature is as inconsistent as the tongue," James seems to sigh as he writes. "Does a fountain send out from the same opening *both* fresh and bitter *water*? Can a fig tree, my brethren, produce olives, or a vine produce figs? Nor *can* salt water produce fresh" (3:11–12).

Inconsistent speech comes from a heart with divided loyalties. Thus we should remain constantly on the alert for this awful problem with the spoken word.

So where does this discussion of the awful problem with the spoken word leave you? Are you a victim? Are there accusing statements from others buried in your heart, statements that periodically surface to rob you of God's best for your life? Do you stand before great possibilities, intimidated by negative statements out of the past? Are you operating on false assumptions based on words you may have only casually overheard or read, but have now come to firmly believe as true about yourself? If you are a victim of the curse of words, read on, and you'll discover how you can be set free.

But before we go back to my family's dinner table, I want to share some exciting news with you. There is a curse that has already been broken!

5

The Curse That Is Already Broken

What if your mother often told you that your eyes were too wide-set and that you ought to devise a way to draw people's attention away from them? "Comb your hair differently, or just do something!" she might say in exasperation, as if such a feat was possible.

Such words bring hurt, frustration and, ultimately, the kind of bitterness that becomes destructive to the human soul. Through your teenage years, you might keep your head ducked in embarrassment and shame. By college, you are angered that your mother is embarrassed over something for which she was actually more responsible than you. Growing into adulthood, you could easily assume that your choice for a life's mate would be limited by what you have now come to see as an affliction. Every morning, as those eyes look back at you from the bathroom mirror, you start out the day with negative thoughts about yourself, laboring under the curse of words.

Finally, you might find it easier just to blame God and turn in anger against Him.

I have heard stories just like the one above from people whose parents expressed an open dislike for their child's physical features, attributes that are more a product of birth than desire. And sometimes it's not so much one's physical appearance that draws negative comments but a personality trait instead. "She's always been a quiet one, keeping to herself." "He's been a show-off since the day he was born." Though sometimes considered as nothing but good-natured teasing, at specific moments of vulnerability such words planted in the heart begin to produce the kind of fruit that debilitates and ultimately devastates a life. Can such a powerful curse be broken?

I WANT TO TELL YOU ABOUT another and far more powerful curse than the curse of words. It is a curse that has already been broken—forever, in fact. Would that encourage you to believe that the specific curse of words with which you are now dealing could actually be conquered? There is such a curse—one of unimaginable power—and it has been broken, and will remain so forever. It is the curse of sin, which is death.

God's Word unequivocally states that all mankind labors under the curse of sin. Such has been the case since our human father, Adam, first sinned in the garden of Eden. From that moment on, every person born out of the union of a man and a woman has inherited the nature of sin. While we can learn how to sin more deviously, sin is not something that we are taught; it is a nature that we possess. We don't become sinners by sinning anymore than a dog becomes a dog by barking. A dog barks because it's a dog. And we sin because we are, in our very nature, sinners.

In His Word, the Bible, God goes to great lengths to make certain we understand that we are sinners. We are all like sheep that have gone astray, lamented the prophet Isaiah (see 53:6). Paul underscored that truth by echoing the sentiments of the psalmist (see Ps. 14:1–3), writing, "There is none righteous, not even one" (Rom. 3:10). The bottom line is this, as Paul concluded: All of us have sinned and come short of the glory of God (see 3:23).

I have met people who have questioned the reality of God, the facts of creation and the Person of Christ. But I have yet to meet a person who, when questioned about it, did not admit that there was sin in his or her life. We not only violate the laws of God; we find it impossible even to abide by the laws we make for ourselves. We are under the curse of sin. And what is the curse, or result, of sin? Here again, God provides us with a clear answer.

"The wages of sin is death" (Rom. 6:23). Death comes in many forms. Physical death is the separation of life from the body. But spiritual death means to be separated from God. And the ultimate tragedy of sin's curse is that, unless a remedy can be found, each one of us will be separated from God for all eternity.

Here is the good news about sin's curse. It has been broken! Jesus Christ, God's Son came to this earth by virtue of a virgin birth. As such, He did not inherit Adam's nature of sin. Because of God's great love for us, Jesus chose willingly to die in your place and mine, taking the curse of sin and death upon Himself. In fact, God's Word tells us that God made Jesus, who knew no sin "to *be* sin on our behalf" (2 Cor. 5:21). Even as He died on the cross, people recalled the Scripture that says, "CURSED IS EVERYONE WHO HANGS ON A TREE" (Gal. 3:13; see also Deut. 21:23).

Peter, one of the Lord's disciples, wrote in vivid language about Christ's death and what it was meant to accomplish. "For Christ also died for sins once for all, *the* just for *the* unjust, so that He might bring us to God, having been put to death in the flesh, but made alive in the spirit" (1 Pet. 3:18).

Because Jesus never sinned, He could die in your place and mine! And because He knew no sin, death and the grave could not hold Him. The resurrection of Jesus was God's way of proving that the curse of sin, which is death, was forever broken. No wonder Paul exclaims in words that almost leap off the printed page, "'O DEATH, WHERE IS YOUR VICTORY? O DEATH, WHERE IS YOUR STING?' The sting of death is sin, and the power of sin is the law; but thanks be to God, who gives us the victory through our Lord Jesus Christ" (1 Cor. 15:55–57).

You can be set free forever from the curse of sin which is death, or eternal separation from God, if you will repent of your sin and receive Christ, by faith, as your Savior, trusting Him as Lord of your life. This is the testimony of the Scripture: "But as many as received Him, to them He gave the right to become children of God, *even* to those who believe in His name, who were born, not of blood nor of the will of the flesh nor of the will of man, but of God" (John 1:12–13).

It's little wonder the account of Jesus' birth, death and resurrection is called the "Good News," or the gospel. Think of it! Because of Jesus, you can be set free from the curse of sin, which is death, and live eternally in heaven with God.

Have you come before God in repentance and faith in Christ, acknowledging Him as your Savior and Lord and receiving His gift of forgiveness and eternal life? If so, you possess three very powerful weapons that enable you to gain victory in every area of life, including victory over the curse of words. Those weapons are:

- **His Word**

- **His Name**

- **His Blood**

Now, would you grant me a small but very important favor? It is urgent for you to understand why each of these three weapons is so powerful. That is why I want to tell you more about each weapon in the following three chapters. Then, we can return to the dinner table where I'll explain how to use each of these weapons to break the curse of words in your life.

They'll save us a place at the table. Trust me!

6

His Word

Many years ago, as part of a Fourth of July Celebration for a church I pastored in Tulsa, Oklahoma, we hosted Captain Howard Rutledge, a US pilot only recently released as a POW from Hanoi's infamous Heartbreak Hotel. All of us listened in rapt attention as Rutledge described the unimaginable cruelties inflicted on him and his fellow inmates over a seven-year period of incarceration. Added to the daily list of sickening physical atrocities were the unrelenting verbal attempts to brainwash the prisoners, attempts to break down both a man's will and spirit through a devious, mind-numbing assortment of ploys. The ultimate objective of brainwashing is for a man to begin thinking of himself as exactly the opposite of who he really is.

You could hear the proverbial pin drop as Rutledge began sharing about the one practice that helped him and his fellow inmates maintain both their sanity and their touch with who they were in truth. He told how, as a young boy in a Southern Baptist Church in Tulsa, Oklahoma, he had memorized various verses of Scripture to be quoted in Sunday school. Other inmates had done the same as young men; and soon they began to share verses with each other, comprising a list that became quite significant.

Did the enemy ultimately succeed in shaping Rutledge into a contorted caricature of the man he really was? "Not at all," said Rutledge. He told how he and the other prisoners took solace in the Word of God, finding encouragement in the truths of the Scripture they'd memorized. Rutledge, who later authored the stirring account of his imprisonment and subsequent release in the book In the Presence of Mine Enemies, *perfectly illustrated how the Word of God can be powerfully employed to break a curse of words in your own life.*

WHAT IS THE TRUTH? It seems that this age-old question surfaced every time Jesus entered Jerusalem. He was determined that men and women would see how truth was always found in God's Word, regardless of what their traditions might assert. On one such instance, Jesus made the following statement about the nature of God's Word and its power to set people free. Turning to those Jews who had believed Him, He said, "If you continue in My word, *then* you are truly disciples of Mine; and you will know the truth, and the truth will make you free" (John 8:31–32).

Jesus' declaration is both astounding and perfectly clear. It was this passage of Scripture that God first brought to my mind on that long drive home. Even as I pleaded with Christ to show me how to be set free from the curse of words, I knew deep within that what God said about me in His Word took precedence over any human assertion. His Word was the ultimate authority, or "true truth" as a friend of mine was accustomed to saying.

Freedom is a product of one's environment. Each of God's creatures is designed to operate freely within a specific environment. Imprisonment, the loss of personal freedom, occurs outside of that environment. A bird, for instance, is not considered free if it is trapped beneath the surface of the water. Nor is a fish considered free if it is taken from its watery home. Birds fly freely in the open, airy spaces, and fish swim freely when they are beneath the surface of the sea.

I knew that when I repented of sin and believed on Christ unto salvation, I had immediately become a new creation in Christ Jesus (see 2 Cor. 5:17). So where was that environment in which this "new creature" could operate with freedom? It was within the Word of God!

Nothing more, and certainly nothing less! As long as I remained within the parameters of God's Word, I could operate with freedom, having no obligation to those outside claims insidiously leveled at me by Satan, the great accuser (see Rev. 12:10).

This simple truth powerfully gripped my heart. I saw that the Word of God took precedence over any accusation, any criticism, and any casual statement I may have overheard—or just always assumed to be true. Anything not said to be true of me in God's Word has no legitimate claim on my life. I am, in very fact, set free to be all that God says is true of me as His child!

When you realize that God's Word is the truth that sets men and women free, you will approach it with fresh enthusiasm and a new set of eyes. You will understand why Paul was so insistent that Timothy, his young protégé, develop a proper appreciation for the powerful nature of God's Word. "All Scripture," Paul wrote to Timothy, "is inspired by God and profitable for teaching, for reproof, for correction, for training in righteousness; so that the man of God may be adequate, equipped for every good work" (2 Tim. 3:16–17).

The 119th Psalm comprises the longest chapter in the Bible. Each of its 176 verses focuses our attention on some aspect of the Bible, God's Word. This psalm is an example of the role God wants His Word to play in your life. By familiarizing yourself with His Word, you will develop a "verbal immune system" that immediately rejects any statement that does not line up with God's truth. No wonder the psalmist offered God his praise by writing "Forever, O LORD, Your word is settled in heaven" (Ps. 119:89). Since God's Word is settled forever in heaven, certainly we should settle down in it today, in our world.

The more you read the Word of God, the more you will see that it is the only environment in which you can live with freedom. In fact, God's plan is for us to live *by* His grace and *in* His Word. Jesus said that by the application of God's Word we can be *in* the world but not *of* the world (see John 17:14–18). On one occasion, Israel's great leader Moses reviewed the manner by which God had led Israel out of Egyptian bondage and supplied their needs while in the wilderness. He reminded the nation of God's singular purpose through it all. God did this, said Moses, so "that He might make you to understand that man does not live by bread alone, but . . . by everything that proceeds out of the mouth of the LORD" (Deut. 8:3). In other words, you and I are to live in the Word of God. Later in this book, I will explain in greater detail how God enabled me to break the curse of words through the power of His Word. However, that would not have been the case had I not possessed at least *some* familiarity with God's Word. It is through Scripture memorization and our meditation on it, that the Word of God becomes of greatest effectiveness in our lives.

How can you employ the Word of God to break a curse of words? We'll get to that in a moment—after we examine the two remaining and very powerful weapons God provides for each one of His children.

7

His Name

As I was finishing up the last of a hearty country breakfast, my great-aunt busied herself at the kitchen sink, snapping beans for Sunday's lunch. She and my grandfather, having both lost their spouses to death, now lived together on my grandfather's farm. They were both almost ninety years of age, and filled with the wisdom that comes from working hard, living right and trusting in God. My grandfather and grandmother had reared eleven children on that farm, all of whom were faithful Christians and who now had their own measure of success. In addition to being a farmer, my grandfather was, for many years, the county judge.

A freshman in college, I stayed in that farmhouse each weekend while pastoring a small mission in the county seat town, nine miles to the south. My Aunt Roxie's cooking was legendary, especially when it came to her fried pies. Her wit and wisdom were rivaled only by my grandfather's, and each weekend,

I soaked it in like a sponge. But I was little prepared for the stern and sobering nature of my aunt's words that morning.

Recounting my grandfather's many years in that area, and the high regard everyone had for him, my aunt turned from the sink, pointed a long finger at me and said, "Listen to me. Your grandfather is loved and respected by everybody in this county. He has always kept his word, gone the second mile, paid his debts on time, and quietly supported every good thing that has happened around here."

I nodded my head in agreement, knowing she was correct.

"So," my aunt continued, "what I'm saying is that your grandfather has left you a great inheritance, the inheritance of a good name. Don't you dare mess up that name." With that, my aunt turned her attention again to snapping the beans piled in the bowl before her.

I sat looking at my plate, lost in thought and determined never to do anything that would bring the slightest bit of disgrace to my grandfather's name. His name was, indeed, powerful in that community. There was virtually nothing I could have asked of anyone that they would not have attempted to do for me because I was Judge Carter's grandson.

But there is a name that is infinitely more powerful than my grandfather's.

THE NAME OF JESUS. The message spoken deep within my heart as I drove homeward that night was not audible, but quite distinct. The name of Jesus. Of course, I thought, I always pray in the name of Jesus. What Christian doesn't? But is there more to this statement than I have always assumed? Is there something about the name of Jesus that I am missing; something that would explain its power? That evening, my meditation on the name of Jesus proved to be one of the most exciting and fruitful experiences of my life's journey with Christ.

My initial thoughts about praying "in Jesus' name" were related to the issue of every genuine Christian's position *in* Christ, and Christ's position *within* the believer. When a person repents and believes in Jesus unto salvation, Christ literally comes to dwell within that person. From His position in us, Christ assures us of our eternal destination. That is why you can say with Paul that it is "Christ in you, the hope of glory!" (Col. 1:27).

Every genuine believer is quite literally in Christ, as well. This is a reality that has breathtaking ramifications. In the name of Jesus, we operate both from a position of security and authority. From this position we are assured of access to the throne of the universe, where, before our Sovereign God, we discover that we are more than heirs of all the privileges of heaven; we are in fact joint heirs with Jesus Himself (see Eph. 3:6).

That truth alone should be enough to encourage any Christian as to the effectiveness and power of prayer. But as I mentioned earlier, I felt that there must be more to the whole issue surrounding the name of Jesus. What more could there be?

In the culture of Christ's day, any reference to a person's name involved more than the mere appellation by which a person was called. A person's name referred to every characteristic involved in making that person unique among all others on the earth. Even today, it remains true in some cultures that to give someone your name is to actually allow them access to your "self." For this reason, people in those cultures are often quite reluctant to give someone their name, reserving that privilege for only the closest of friends.

As previously mentioned, such was the case in our Lord's day and in the Judeo-Christian culture associated with the Bible. For this reason, it is not simply the name J-E-S-U-S that is so very powerful; it is everything about the person who bears that name. For example, the third commandment strictly forbids taking the name of the Lord our God in vain (see Exod. 20:7). But surely, as important as that is, the commandment must be more than a mere prohibition against using God's name as an epithet or curse word. Understood fully, the third commandment is a prohibition against taking God lightly or irreverently—by any means and in any setting. In other words, the name of Jesus is synonymous with the Person of Jesus.

Did you know that God specifically states that His agenda for your life and mine includes all that is required to make us like His Son, Jesus? What could be more encouraging than to know that God is actually working within us for this specific purpose? And God is so confident in the success of His agenda that He is already willing to give us His name. He knows what we are, what we are becoming, and what we will ultimately become.

Look at the testimony of the Scripture. Paul, for instance, is eager for us to understand this great purpose of God when he writes that, from before time, it was God's determined purpose that His children be "conformed to the image of His Son" (Rom. 8: 29). Writing to the Christians in Philippi, he again refers to God's agenda in making us like Jesus, reminding us that God is actually doing the work within us, "both to will and to work for *His* good pleasure" (Phil. 2: 13). In other words, God is giving us both the desire and the ability to become Christlike. When the character of Christ is evident in a person's life, it is called the "fruit of the Spirit" (Gal. 5:22). Fruit is nothing more than the outward expression of the inward nature of Christ who dwells within us.

Now, here is the truth that God began to unfold in my heart while driving west on Interstate 40: Regardless of those words of accusation or insinuation, either spoken or overheard in days past, whether actually true or not, God is powerfully at work within each true child of His, not only forgiving our sin, but also conforming us to the image of His Son, Jesus. Even when we are failing in our repeated efforts to change, He is quietly, insistently drawing us into the kind of fellowship with Him that will result in our becoming like Jesus. That is why we can break free from the curse of words in Jesus' name.

But there is one more weapon left in the arsenal we have been given. We must understand it thoroughly in order for it to be employed effectively. And in some ways this weapon is the most potent.

8

His Blood

For many years I had the privilege of pastoring a church in a military community. That church is neighbor to one of the largest air logistics bases in the nation. I still reside in that community and relish the privilege of living among so many that are willing to give their lives, if necessary, that our nation might remain a free and sovereign republic.

Situated as I am in this community, I remain ever mindful that our freedoms have been purchased for us by men and women who were willing to place themselves "in harms way" so that their families, and indeed our entire nation, might remain free from the rule of tyrants.

When the Fourth of July rolls around each year, our community has more than its share of patriotic services, memorials, parades and fireworks displays. I cherish those moments as a way to express my gratitude, and I encourage them as an ef-

fective means of keeping our nation's history alive in the minds of the coming generations.

But our freedoms are not simply philosophical ideas, bought at the costly expense of the lifeblood of countless others, only to be recorded and periodically memorialized. Freedom must be kept alive by its daily exercise. It must be protected, utilized, remembered and reviewed. What we do not use, we will lose. And so freedom must be practiced—wisely, carefully and ardently.

Christ's willing submission of Himself to the cross, over two thousand years ago, purchased for every believer a freedom from the dominion of sin that is also to be practiced—faithfully, wisely, passionately.

MAYBE YOU HAVE HEARD THE TERM "the blood of Jesus" launched carelessly into the atmosphere when there is the slightest hint of spiritual warfare. An acquaintance of mine irreverently says about virtually everything that seems confusing to him, "Well, brothers, let's just put it all under the blood." However, to an understanding believer in Christ, any discussion of the blood of Jesus involves a journey over the most sacred ground of the Christian faith. I have often thought of the blood of Jesus as the most powerful arrow in the

Christian's quiver. Driving westward toward Oklahoma City that night many years ago, my thoughts about the blood of Jesus were not primarily related to the theology of Christ's death or *why* Jesus, as God's Son, died in order to pay for our sin. I was thinking, instead, about the personal, practical, contemporary application of Jesus' death: In what way could the remarkable power of the crucifixion of Jesus be applied *today* to bring victory over sin? To be even more specific, how could what Jesus did over two thousand years ago bring me present release from the curse of words and the sinful behavior it prompted?

For too many of us, all thoughts of the Lord's crucifixion are lost somewhere in the past tense. We focus our attention on what the crucifixion accomplished, that is, the satisfactory payment for the sin of mankind. But Christ's death, consummated in the shedding of His life's blood, was much more than the painful outpouring of His passion, though that is agonizingly true enough. The cross must be seen as something more than merely the gruesome location for Christ's suffering.

The cross was the terminus, the ending of our Savior's life, the point where all the stored up wrath of God against sin was suddenly and violently released on the Messiah, God's chosen Servant. On the cross, as He willingly poured out His life, He (Christ) who knew no sin became sin for us, so that we (sinners) might become the righteousness of God through faith in Him (see 2 Cor. 5:21). On these facts, most of us reading this would generally agree.

What we desperately need, however, is a fresh grasp of the incredible power that continues to spring from the reality of Jesus' crucifixion. We know what Jesus death *has* accomplished in paying for our sin—past, present and future. But we desire to experience what it can *now* accomplish in terms of daily, moment-by-moment victory over sin, including victory over the curse of words. How can that happen?

When John writes that God is Light, and then urges us to walk in the Light, he is referring to the fact that we can live in daily, intimate fellowship with the Father (see 1 John 1:5–7). John makes it clear that this involves seeing our sin as sin and calling it so, and then confronting sin, confessing it humbly and claiming Christ's forgiveness (see 1:9).

But notice what happens when we walk in the Light. John tells us that we will begin walking in fellowship with other believers who are also eager for unhindered fellowship with the Father. What an encouragement that is to us! But there is more! Walking in the Light enables us to enjoy the dynamic, moment-by-moment experience of being cleansed from all sin by the blood of Jesus, God's Son (see 1 John 1:6–7).

Notice John's careful choice of words in this passage: "If we say that we have fellowship with Him and *yet* walk in the darkness, we lie and do not practice the truth; but if we walk in the Light as He Himself is in the Light, we have fellowship with one another, and the blood of Jesus His Son cleanses us from all sin."

This is the power of the cross! Two thousand years ago, by His death, Christ paid the penalty of our sin. In simple faith we can turn from sin, trust in Christ and claim that payment as our own, receiving God's forgiveness and eternal life.

But, here is how the blood of Jesus, the sacrifice of His life for yours and mine, enables us to be set free from the moment-by-moment rule of sin over our lives, including sins related to the curse of words. Paul said, "If we have died with Christ [i.e., if we are identified with the freedom and forgiveness Christ purchased for us on the cross two thousand years ago], we believe that we shall also live with Him [today, right now]" (Rom. 6:8). That is why we can assert with him that sin no longer has dominion, or mastery, over us" (6:14). There is no sin in your life or mine, including the defeated resignation to a curse of words, that was not overcome on the cross. No sin wriggled beneath Calvary unscathed or untouched by His blood and its atoning work. What remains is for the true believer in Christ to exercise the potent weapon placed in his hand—the power of the blood of Jesus.

Now that you know the three weapons God places at the disposal of every believer, it is time for you to join the battle and gain the victory. My family is waiting for you at the table. And, like you, they are waiting to break the curse of words.

9

Breaking the Curse of Words

One at a time, those five curses, driven first into submission by the Word of God, then unable to stand when confronted by the name of Jesus, now began to crumble and fade into nothingness at the foot of the cross where Jesus' life was poured out for cleansing on my behalf.

God brought me freedom from the curse of those words—and I began to sing.

"NOW THAT YOU HAVE BEEN SO PATIENT, I think its time for me to tell you what happened to me last night." With those words, I began pouring out my heart to my family, telling them the way the Lord had shown me how to break the curse of words by using the three weapons He has made available to me: His Word, His name and His blood.

To say that I was excited would have been a vast understatement. Eager would have been a better word, because I could sense that genuine victory was within my grasp. As my car forged through the night, outwardly indistinguishable from the others on the road, a fierce battle was being waged within. Praying that God would give me grace, I mentally began seizing each of the curses by the neck, dragging them out into the open where I would force a confrontation with the three weapons in my arsenal of faith—the Word of God, the name of Jesus and the blood of Christ.

First, I brought each of the five statements before the Word of God. Reflecting on each one, I asked this question: *Is there anywhere in God's Word where it is written that this statement is inevitably true of me?*

Searching the Bible verses I could recall, I asked the Lord to reveal the truth about me. I wanted to know if it was God's opinion of me that was being verbalized in the words of those five statements, or the devil's. I almost laughed when I discovered that, not only did God's Word *not* label me with any of those five accusations, it actually included frequent, strong and pointed statements to the contrary.

Frankly, I was more than a bit chagrined at my own childish foolishness. Why had I never challenged these statements before? Why was it that I had allowed these statements to ride over me, roughshod, simply assuming they were unquestionably true? Why had I lived defeated for so many years, finally growing so weary of failed resolutions that, deep within, I harbored serious doubts about God's ability to change me? Why had I walled off certain areas of my life from others, rejecting all honest scrutiny and healthy advice offered by sincere friends, including my own wife?

The more I thought about it the more ludicrous it seemed. You must remember that I grew up in an atmosphere that was overwhelmingly positive, affirming and supportive! I could not imagine the similar struggles that others must have been going through in the congregations I had pastored. What of the children who rarely heard from their parents unless they were being reprimanded for something wrong or disappointing? How many spouses had resigned themselves to being on the short end of a constant comparison with the men and women where their own husband or wife worked?

What of adults who lived self-consciously and ashamed because of taunts about characteristics over which they had no control? What of husbands whose wives repeatedly mocked them among their peers because of unmet goals and broken promises? And what of those wives who had just finally given up on enjoying an evening out because they were inevitably the butt of every joke? What about the endless number of people who just grew up with the assumption that they couldn't sing, play an instrument, speak publicly, succeed on the athletic field, or excel as a scientist, businessman, artist, minister or counselor? What about those who had been told that their physical challenge would spoil their chances for a happy life?

I wondered how much potential would forever remain untouched in the lives of countless men and women because parents, siblings, teachers, friends, work associates and others had unknowingly uttered hurtful words in a careless moment. The brush and palette of their tongue, so capable of pointing spirits to the sky, had been used instead to paint small, weak and pitiful pictures on the walls of a waiting heart. Though I was personally rejoicing at the prospect of impending victory, I began to cry, thinking of all those who had yet to hear that they could be liberated from the sinister, debilitating effects of the curse of words.

"On the authority of God's Word, I break you!" I shouted—so loudly in fact that I startled myself. One at a time, I addressed each of the statements as I brought them before the Word of God and found them wanting.

Assured that God's Word has power of attorney over every devilish accusation, I began to feel their grip on me diminish. My excitement and eagerness only increased.

"Now," I spoke aloud, addressing each of the five curses again, "I want to bring each of you before the name of Jesus, that strong name which stands for the very Person of Christ. There, in His presence, I will discover if you are indeed a true reflection of Christ. He is conforming me to His image, according to Romans 8:29, and if you are not like Christ, I will break your authority in the name of Jesus, whose I am as a child of God."

It seemed as if those curses wanted to run and hide at the name of Jesus. As I called them out by name, I was overwhelmed by how unlike Jesus each of those five statements actually was, especially the ones that started with "You are just like . . . " or "You will never . . . ." Why had I never challenged these statements in this manner before? Was it because I had such great respect for those who said them? Was it because I had heard them in a moment of spiritual weakness or vulnerability?

I remembered Paul's expression, the statement we sometimes call his magnificent obsession. Paul said that, in addition to knowing Christ and the fellowship of His sufferings, even if it meant being conformed to Christ's death, he passionately desired to experience the "power of His resurrection" (Phil. 3:10). For a moment I was stunned by the recollection of the power exhibited in the resurrection of Jesus.

Jesus truly died on the cross. He was not *almost* dead. He was not *in a coma*. He was not *in a drunken stupor*, or *out on drugs*. Jesus was not *pretending* to be dead. He *was* dead. Nothing short of Christ's absolute death would do to pay for the sin of mankind. Jesus was dead when He was placed in that tomb beneath Golgotha, and He remained that way until early in the morning on the third day following His death.

But on that third day, God the Father raised up God the Son, as a testimony that sin and death and the grave could not hold the body of Christ. Think of the power of the resurrection! The power to take a lifeless form, to infuse life into it, to raise it up unto life eternal, and then to do the same for every person who will follow Christ as Savior! That is resurrection power!

"Now," I asked, "what is there in my life that cannot be changed by that kind of power and conformed to the very image of Christ? Absolutely nothing! And God the Spirit is at work conforming me into the image of His Son. In fact, if a true Christian has anything in his life that is not like Jesus, God is at work to remove it. I can only hang on to un-Christlikeness by a deliberate, intentional choice of my will, because God is making me like Jesus. By his blood Christ paid for my sin, and by His resurrected life He is empowering me to overcome it.

"In the strong name of Jesus, whose I am, who lives in me, and who is causing me to become like Him, I break the curse of these words." By this time I was rejoicing. Tears were running down my cheeks as I began to experience a freedom I had not known for years.

Now it was time for me to go to Calvary.

Jeannie and I had been privileged to enjoy numerous trips to Israel, but no experience for me could surpass one that occurred at Calvary in 1974. Eager to learn all I could of Israel, I had traveled there alone, meeting with my host from time to time but spending most of each day apart in the countryside. While in Jerusalem, I had made my way alone to Gordon's Calvary, one of the places purported to be the actual site of Jesus' crucifixion, subsequent burial, and resurrection.

Throughout that day, I had remained quietly in that serene garden shadowed by Golgotha. I had listened for almost six hours as guides sponsored by Great Britain's Garden Tomb Society shared the facts related to Christ's Passion. As each group had arrived at the tomb, the guides had related the specific details of

Christ's crucifixion, burial and resurrection. While an impressive argument could have been made as to the authenticity of the site, I was not there for the purpose of argument. The power of the cross was the one thing gripping my heart that day, riveting my attention to the events described by the guides. I had not been the only attentive person there that day, as evidenced by the hundreds whose eyes brimmed with tears as their hearts were stirred upon hearing the story of God's love. Most of us there were living testaments of the power of the blood!

Now, years later and alone in the car with those thoughts of Calvary filling my heart, I mentally dragged each of those five curses to the cross. Those curses were already reeling from their encounter with the Word of God and reduced to impotence by the name of Jesus. But up the hill I trudged, dragging them up, up, up Calvary to the very foot of the cross. Once again my heart was filled with a sense of impending victory. "Tell me," I virtually shouted, "did you escape the atoning work of Christ? Has the blood of Christ not touched and conquered you, that blood of Jesus that cleanses us from all unrighteousness?"

One at a time, those five curses, driven first into submission by the Word of God, then unable to stand when confronted by the name of Jesus, now began to crumble and fade into nothingness at the foot of the cross where Jesus' life was poured out for cleansing on my behalf.

God brought me freedom from the curse of those words—and I began to sing.

10

My Appeal

Your speech ultimately tells the truth about what kind of person you are. Do the people nearest to you really hear from you the kind of speech that indicates a heart that has been changed by the grace of God? Is it assuming too much to expect that they believe you have a changed heart even though your speech rarely reflects the grace of God? God is eager to change your heart, and both you and your world need it desperately.

IT HAS NOW BEEN MANY YEARS since that night in early summer when God showed me the awful reality of what I have called the curse of words. As you have read, my intention is in no way to deny the fact that Christ's death and subsequent resurrection to eternal life make it possible for all who will call on His name to be delivered from the curse of sin, which is death. My terminology only echoes that of James who has stated matter-of-factly that with our tongue we both *bless* our Lord and Father and *curse* men (see James 3:9).

We can each accept the reality that it is possible to labor under false conceptions—what I have previously called negative and demeaning pictures, painted on the walls of our hearts by the accuser's use of someone's tongue. While such a reality may explain a less-than-effective life, it in no way excuses it. By the grace of God each of us is to be all that we can be. "By the grace of God," writes Paul, "I am what I am" (1 Cor. 15:10).

Over these past several years, literally hundreds (if not thousands) of individuals have come to realize the joy of being set free from the curse of words. I do not believe I have ever addressed this issue publicly without being met afterwards by any number of people who want to tell me their personal story related to a curse of words. Shortly, you will read the powerful testimony of just such an individual.

For many people, the idea has simply never occurred to them that their present behavior could be so closely tied to a statement (or statements) overheard at some vulnerable moment in the past. Yet even a brief refection can often bring that moment into vivid clarity. Words are powerful. That said, I'd like to use these next few pages to discharge a solemn, twofold responsibility.

Please do yourself the favor of reading these pages carefully. Otherwise the message of this book, though true and powerful, will simply end with you. As soon as possible, seek an avenue by which you can implement the two-fold appeal that I will make.

Now, what is that appeal?

First, don't be afraid to ask God to reveal to you what statements may have had either a negative or positive impact on your life today. For those that are negative, consider them in the light of the truths presented in this small book. Break the curse of those words, and experience the freedom that comes to those who "walk in the Light." No more explanation is needed than what has been given in the previous pages.

Where you find that you have been blessed by positive and encouraging words, do all you can to express gratitude both to God and, if possible, to those who shared those words with you. You have an opportunity to make lives better, both yours and theirs, and it will cost you little, if anything.

Do you not owe a debt of gratitude to those who helped properly set the compass of your life? And shouldn't you use your tongue to bless them as they used theirs to bless you? Gratitude always lifts everyone's heart higher.

Here is the *second* appeal, and one that is quite serious in nature. Will you take time to consider how you have used your tongue to either encourage others or tear them down? Are there important people in your life, such as your family members, who cannot recall any word of encouragement that you have ever shared with them? Or, are you known for the manner in which you cannot allow anything to pass without some negative word from you?

Jesus, the incarnate Word of God, said that it is out of the abundance of a man's heart that he speaks (see Luke 6:45). In other words, what you talk about a little, you think about a lot. You can sugarcoat your speech for a while, but ultimately your tongue will tell on you. What does your speech say about the condition of your heart?

In the end, people will conclude that your speech makes them either better or bitter. Is it possible that you need to ask Christ to change your heart? That is something He is well able to do. He is eager, in fact, to do it. Then, having experienced the forgiveness of God, you can ask others to forgive you for the wrong manner in which you have used your tongue. Their eagerness to do so will probably surprise you.

Jesus once went into the house of a man who was notorious for his sin and dishonesty. In fact, the man was simply a selfish puppet of the Roman government, and he often used his position to make life miserable for others. The Scriptures do not tell us this, but it is quite possible that this man may have been so often mocked because of his small stature that he was using his position to get back at people. He had such a bad reputation that even Jesus was criticized for going to be a guest in his house.

But something happened in the heart of this man. Jesus called it "salvation." It was a radical change for this man. Do you know how people first knew of this change? It was by what he said! His changed heart was revealed by his speech. He spoke publicly of his new intentions, saying he would give half of his possessions to the poor, and if he had cheated anyone, he would repay them four times over (see Luke 19:8).

Something wonderful happened to this man whose name was Zaccheus! First, his heart was changed by the grace of God. Then, his speech revealed that changed heart. Later, his actions certified the reality of a changed heart.

Your speech ultimately tells the truth about what kind of person you are. Do the people nearest to you really hear from you the kind of speech that indicates a heart that has been changed by the grace of God? Is it assuming too much to expect that they believe you have a changed heart even though your speech rarely reflects the grace of God? God is eager to change your heart, and both you and your world need it desperately.

Now, I want to tell you one more story.

Epilogue

SEVERAL WEEKS LATER, the pavement was again beating out its rhythm beneath the wheels of my automobile. This time, however, I was not lost in thought, but excitedly sharing with a friend my newly discovered truth about breaking the curse of words. We were on our way to a neighboring state where I would be speaking that evening and he would be visiting with relatives.

For you to fully grasp the significance of what you are about to read, I need to tell you about my friend. First, he is a genuinely good man and a good friend, as close to me, in fact, as my brothers. We attended college together, roomed in the same house, traveled in a folk-singing group, and conducted revivals together while in college.

Later, we commuted together for three years while attending seminary. And then, on two different occasions, we were blessed to work together on the same church staff. My friend is an incredibly effective communicator, a sound expositor of God's Word and a man possessed with a passion for souls.

I truly love my friend and his family. And I have great admiration for him, the clarity of his call to the ministry, his character and his conviction. I have watched him closely for over fifty years now and would say, as Jesus said of Nathanael, that in him can be found "no deceit" (John 1:47). He is a man of utmost integrity, possessing a work ethic that few could ever match. To top it off, my friend is brilliant, so much so that many of us secretly believe he possesses a photographic memory. This is my friend.

As I excitedly poured out my story, telling him about my nighttime journey across Oklahoma, the dinner meeting with my family and the incredible sense of freedom that came from breaking the curse of words, I noticed that he began sinking lower and lower into the seat of my automobile. Looking at him out of the corner of my eye, I could tell he was deep in thought.

Finally, when he could hold the words back no longer, he spoke up. "I've got one," he said. "I have a curse of words." Then he told me a story about a life event I knew nothing of at all.

My friend recalled those days in college when we were both ministering in small south Arkansas towns. He was a student pastor, the first in a church that literally had to make an office for him out of a broom closet.

It was in that office, he told me, that he became the unwitting victim of the curse of words.

Early one morning, two church secretaries were standing outside the door of his "office," unaware that he was just inside. The two ladies were discussing the travels of their pastor, lamenting the fact that he seemed to be out of town quite a bit.

"Well," snorted one of the secretaries, "I'll tell you this about our youth pastor." (She actually called his name.) "He don't [sic] know nothing about preaching, but at least he's always here!"

"I concluded at that moment," said my friend, "that I had nothing to bring to the ministry but to 'always be there,' and I have almost ruined my health fulfilling that role." He then went on to tell of family vacations cut short, journeys through the night to attend the most insignificant of events, constant excuses to his disappointed wife and children, explaining that he just "always had to be there." Here was a man whose life's compass had been set by the unknowing and careless statement of a disgruntled secretary.

I'm happy to say that my friend has broken the curse of those words.

Can the same be said of you?

PUBLICATIONS

Fort Washington, PA 19034

This book is published by CLC Publications, an outreach of CLC Ministries International. The purpose of CLC is to make evangelical Christian literature available to all nations so that people may come to faith and maturity in the Lord Jesus Christ. We hope this book has been life changing and has enriched your walk with God through the work of the Holy Spirit. If you would like to know more about CLC, we invite you to visit our website:

www.clcusa.org

To know more about the remarkable story of the founding of CLC International we encourage you to read:

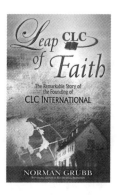

LEAP OF FAITH

Norman Grubb

Paperback

Size 5^1/$_4$ x 8, Pages 248

ISBN: 978-0-87508-650-7

ISBN (*e-book*): 978-1-61958-055-8

Hearing God in the Midst of Your Struggles

THE UNWANTED GIFT

Tom Elliff

In this book, Tom Elliff shares how he and his late wife, Jeannie, came to view their toughest challenge as a gift. Through biblical study and reflection on a personal trial, he demonstrates how to accept that hardships bring life's greatest measure of God's grace and power. Our most painful problems, though unwanted, can truly be gifts from God.

Hardback
Size 5 x 7, Pages 102
ISBN: 978-1-61958-234-7
ISBN (*e-book*): 978-1-61958-235-4

THE PATHWAY TO GOD'S PRESENCE

Tom Elliff

The Pathway to God's Presence encourages those who feel they have lost the sense of God's presence in their lives and wish for restoration. Examining the Old Testament account of Moses and the children of Israel, the book highlights the distinction between "God's provision and His presence."

Paperback

Size 4¹/4 x 7, Pages 140

ISBN (*mass market*): 978-1-61958-156-2

ISBN (*trade paper*): 978-1-61958-170-8

ISBN (*e-book*): 978-1-61958-157-9

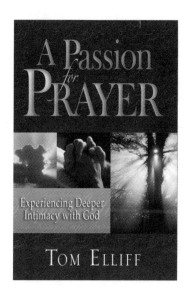

A PASSION FOR PRAYER

Tom Elliff

Of all the disciplines of the Christian life, prayer is perhaps the most neglected. Yet Jesus' brief earthly life was permeated with it. *A Passion for Prayer* seeks to help you develop—or deepen—your communion with God. Drawing on personal experience and God's Word, Pastor Tom Elliff shares principles for daily coming before the throne of grace.

Paperback
Size 5^1/4 x 8, Pages 252
ISBN: 978-1-936143-03-0
ISBN (*e-book*): 978-1-936143-26-9